JOCELYN KERR HOLDING

STENCIL STYLE

Ideas and Projects to Transform your Home

WARD LOCK

CONTENTS

PREFACE

My purpose in writing this book is to encourage and inspire all would-be stencillers –
and in particular those who have never even thought of putting a stencil brush into a
pot of paint – to try their hand at so easy a decorative art.
All the essential materials such as brushes, paints and ready-cut stencils can easily be
found at any good art store. This is encouraging for those of us not totally familiar with
the world of paints. My task is one of teaching stencilling in its most basic form and
then taking it to the limit of its possibilities: the trompe-l'œil. Many books have already
been written on stencilling and many wonderful interiors shown. For the most part,
however, it may not have been totally clear to the reader how these glorious scenes
were realised. I propose to show the reader every step of the way exactly how an effect
is created and which materials are used to obtain it.
   I wish to "draw out" the artist in everyone, to help the reader develop and exercise
     his or her flair for design and colour as we proceed.
       To complete your stencilling techniques, I have included a chapter on
         broken colour effects, such as sponging, ragging and colourwashing.
           These effects will be a tremendous help when stencilling natural
             wood objects or furniture. At the end of the book I have
               illustrated a wide variety of stencils from our collection.
                 There are the typically country-style and the more classic
                 Greek and Roman designs.

INTRODUCTION

It is of no great surprise that stencilling is an extremely popular craft; no special painting ability is required and the necessary steps to produce excellent results can be learnt in an afternoon's lesson.

The art of stencilling, therefore, gives ample opportunity to those who try it, to develop and experiment their creative instincts through the use of pre-cut stencils, together with a wide choice of acrylic colours.

I first discovered stencilling on a trip to London in the 1980s. I happened to be browsing in a department store when I noticed an easel displaying a large stencil design. Close by were brushes and paints and a fascinating brochure illustrating designs and stencilled interiors. I could hardly contain my curiosity long enough to ask an assistant for more details and a quick "how to do" demonstration. As the design materialised in front of my eyes I knew that this was the magic I had been looking for; something that was truly simple, that could be enjoyed by everyone and used in interior decoration.

I bought two brushes, six paints and two stencils. My next move was to contact the foremost authority on stencilling in England, Carolyn Warrender. Carolyn was the owner of a stencil shop in Chelsea. Our subsequent meeting let to a collaboration that would bring stencilling to Italy. In 1989 I set up a shop in Milan similar to Carolyn's in London, selling her stencils and teaching her "dry-brush" technique, the method preferred by the majority of able stencillers.

In this book I hope to have illustrated and explained in the simplest way possible, with step-by-step procedures, ideas for home decorations in which stencilling plays a major role. I trust that these fun techniques will offer my readers many hours of pleasant occupation and creativity.

TECHNIQUE

MATERIALS NEEDED

The proper materials are essential in order to obtain the stunning results illustrated here, with the minimum experimentation.
Almost all efforts at this art produce good to very good results straight away, but so many that I have seen could have been improved by a few clever hints and the use of materials expressly designed for stencilling.
"Please be advised that some materials contain toxic substances: they should be used with the greatest care and following the manufacturer's instructions".

PRE-CUT STENCILS

A stencil can be cut from any sheet of plastic, but it would not wholly satisfy our requirements. When stencilling a design, the "thickness" of the plastic would result in a rim around the edges, causing unsightly smudging. This problem very often occurs when using other materials such as Manila card or cardboard. Many of the first commercial stencils were cut from acetate, but although lightweight and thin, acetate is not tear-proof and tends to split, especially in places where bridges are narrow.
By far the most satisfactory material from which to cut a stencil is "mylar". Treated with polyester, this material is virtually tear-proof and indestructible. Mylar comes in a suitable lightweight version and adheres perfectly to the surface. We have affirmed that stencil film should be as thick as possible, but there are limits to the "floppiness" of stencil film. This problem could be experienced when using stencil with long, thin mobile bridges (the film would roll continuously, making your work laborious).
A practical test when choosing a pre-cut stencil is to run one's finger over the cut-out part and "feel" the two levels: if there is little or no difference, the stencil should work well. Edges will be well-defined and smudging will not occur.

PAINTS

ACRYLIC PAINTS: Acrylics are quick-drying water-based paints. When dry they form an opaque plastic-like coating that is completely waterproof over the surface. Acrylics are especially suited to stencilling since they dry as quickly as you can work, giving you ample opportunity to apply different shades one over the other without the two mixing. Acrylics come in two different types, one for all hard surfaces and one for fabrics only.

CERAMIC PAINTS: Ceramic paints have a solvent base and a liquid fluidity. They are best suited to non-porous surfaces such as tiles, formica, plastic, metal, glass and the like. Because ceramic paints are more liquid than acrylics, it is best to stencil using very little paint and a quick dabbing movement. When the first application becomes "tacky", repeat the process so as to build up the colour gradually. Ceramic paint for stencilling cannot be fired, so it is wise not to use stringent cleaning products (i.e. dishwasher detergents) for cleaning decorated items.

GLASS PAINTS: Also solvent-based, glass paints tend to be thick and gluey. The same method of application is used for glass paints as for ceramics. Do not dilute the paint, use very little and build up the colour with each application. They generally take at least 24 hours to dry (in a relatively dust-free room). The objects to be painted must be completely free of grease spots, so first wash them carefully in luke-warm water and then dry them in a cloth dipped in alcohol. With this type of paint, it is often necessary to apply a second coat, to give the colour more body. If you like, you may also use water-based glass paint.

BRUSHES

For stencil paints to successfully create a shaded delicate effect, the brush is the instrument with which we can engineer the result and dose the paint. Brushes should have long, soft bristles (though not too soft) and be extremely flexible. In this way we can increase the pressure on the brush for a darker result, or put virtually no pressure at all for a lighter effect.

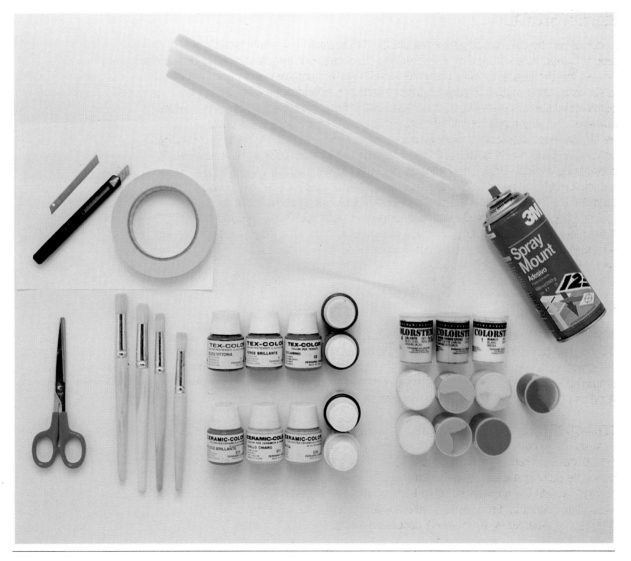

CUTTING YOUR STENCIL

Always cut your stencil on a hard surface, such as glass. The incision made by your cutting knife should be clean and decisive. Tilt the blade so as to use only the tip. Guide the knife with your index finger, always cutting towards you and turning your stencil around to accommodate curves and circles, rather than turning your knife in an awkward direction. In this way the shape is neat; rough edges should be carefully trimmed. If you are using mylar you may trace your design onto the reverse side of the film and cut directly on the shiny side. If instead you use card, smooth the edges with sandpaper.

When you cut your border or running frieze pattern, make sure that the design matches up properly when turned round, guaranteeing a continuous pattern.

GOTHIC BORDER

Shown here is a simple border motif found in a book of Gothic bas-reliefs. A motif such as this can easily be transformed into a stencil if you think of it as being composed of various elements. We "take it apart" and then recompose it, placing the elements as near as possible to each other without touching. Seen in white are the "bridges" that hold the stencil together.

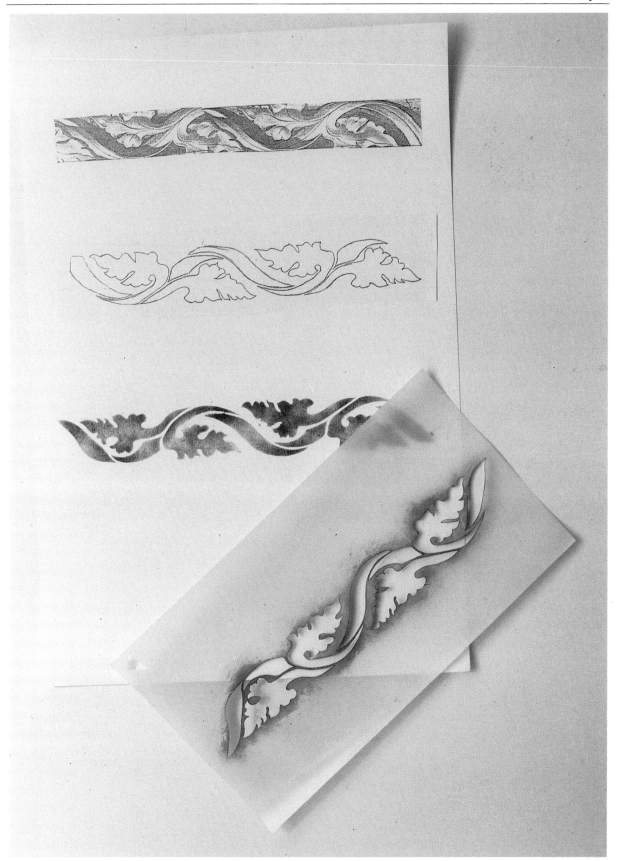

POPPY

An easy way to cut a stencil is to trace a drawing like this poppy onto tracing paper or onto the reverse side of your stencil film.

Look at the design and imagine it coming apart in pieces: each piece or element will be separated by a bridge.

Do not put in any unnecessary bridges. It is true these hold the stencil together, but they also break up the design, making it disjointed, so it is advisable to keep them to a minimum. Make your bridges narrow but not too fragile.
Use a sharp craft knife to cut your stencil.

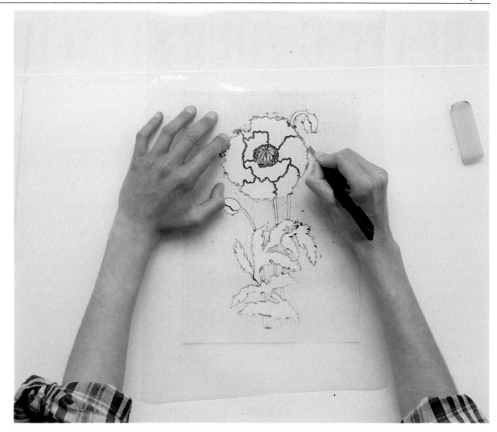

Colour your stencil drawing using soft tones, and delicately dab a lighter contrasting colour on the petals to add brilliance and simulate movement.

CREATING YOUR STENCIL

Use paints that are made specifically for stencil work. Other types of acrylic paints, although compatible with stencil paints, need to be diluted with water and do not contain the drying agent essential for neat, smudgeless edges. Your paint should always be completely dry so that you can easily reposition one or two overlays without fear of smudging. Do not use fabric paint on hard surfaces, or hard-surface paint on fabric. The two paints are similar, but the consistency of fabric paints is more liquid and not suitable for walls, whereas hard-surface paints are thicker and tend to clog the fibres of the fabric. When stencilling fabric choose a 100% natural fibre cloth. Natural fibres absorb the paint, whereas synthetic fibres will repel the paint and hence require dry-cleaning and cannot be hand-washed. Your stencil brush should have long, soft bristles and be flexible. This flexibility is needed for the shading techniques. We push down on the brush for a darker shade and use less pressure for a lighter shade.

Lightly spray the reverse side of your stencil with adhesive spray. If your film has no mat side, then keep one side exclusively for spraying and the other only for painting.

Affix the stencil firmly to your surface, checking that all parts adhere perfectly. Dip the tip of your brush in the paint.

Now clean your brush on kitchen paper using a circular movement; this will rid the brush of excess paint and at the same time spread the paint evenly over the bristles.

Having cleaned your brush well on absorbent paper, you should now have only the thinnest layer of paint on the bristles. The only mistake first-time stencillers make is to use too much paint on the brush.

With circular strokes in both directions, gradually colour in all the areas, keeping your strokes flowing and decisive.

If the design has a large area to be coloured, say, a vase, be careful not to start here, as the colour will be far too emphatic where the brush was freshly loaded with paint.

Once done, gently detach the stencil from the paper.

FRIEZES

Borders are by far the most popular wall decorations; yet however easy a simple frieze might seem, there are a few fundamental rules to bear in mind.

Before you start look carefully at the wall, check whether there is a niche, or if the ceiling slopes. See also if there any architectural irregularities, like a protruding section. Your frieze will have to accommodate these inconveniences.

The drawings below illustrate some of the effects you can obtain with simple borders.

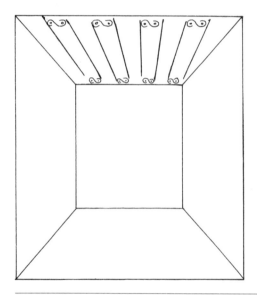

*(left)
A motif between the beams "shortens" the length of the ceiling.*

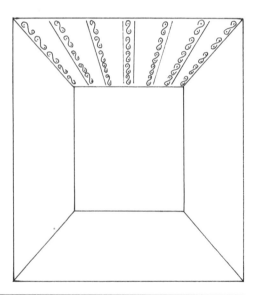

*(right)
A border along the length of the beams accentuates the length, visually elongating the ceiling.*

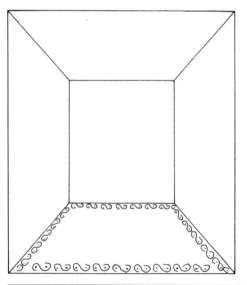

*(left)
A stencilled floor delineates the perimeter and draws the eye downwards.*

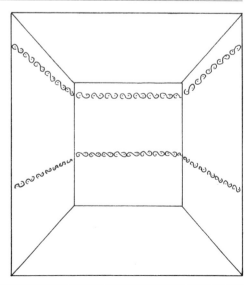

*(right)
A border slightly clear of the ceiling and another at the dado rail tend to bring a high ceiling closer.*

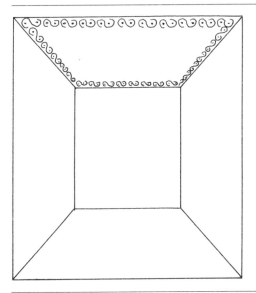

(left)
A stencil pattern on the ceiling makes it seem higher.

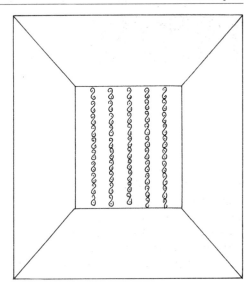

(right)
Stencilling a single wall in a room will help make it seem a little closer.

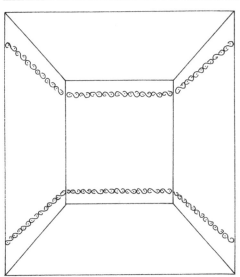

(left)
A border just below the ceiling and another at skirting-board level delineates and draws the attention to the central portion of the wall.

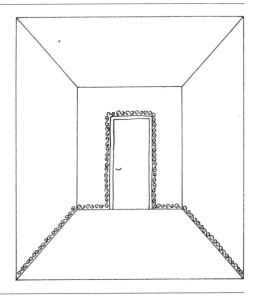

(right)
Movement is created where a border travels up and round the door, and then continues along the skirting.

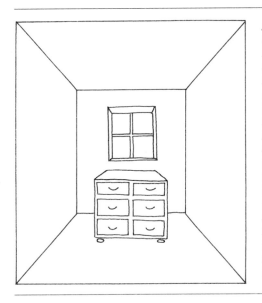

A small room (left) is made to seem larger when opposite walls are stencilled with vertical borders. Up-and-down stripes (right) heighten the ceiling and bring the walls together.
The picture on the left shows the effect before stencilling and the one on the right shows how it looks afterwards.

RAMAGE

A certain amount of courage is needed when we first dip the paintbrush into a pot of paint and start decorating one of our sitting-room walls. Do not let it worry you: just remember that you are allowing your personality to shine through! You are creating a composition that is your own interpretation of images seen or invented. Ramage is the effect created by using stencils of a trailing vine or a climbing plant. If you take a moment to look at a plant, you will notice that some leaves are hidden behind others, some branches are near, while others are only partly visible. Try to give your composition a sense of contrast by superimposing the elements. Your ramage will be greatly improved if you trace a pattern on the wall first, indicating the direction of your creeper. Stand back and visualise your composition. Do not rely on your sense of direction while stencilling.

GRAPES AND BUTTERFLIES

Since a climbing plant must cling and grow, look for a location where a creeper could extend its branches artistically. Such a place could be an arch, around a window, along a balcony, or up a winding staircase. Remember that some parts of the drawing lie behind others: one leaf will hide another, whereas others will peep out from behind bunches of grapes, and so on, as with a real plant.

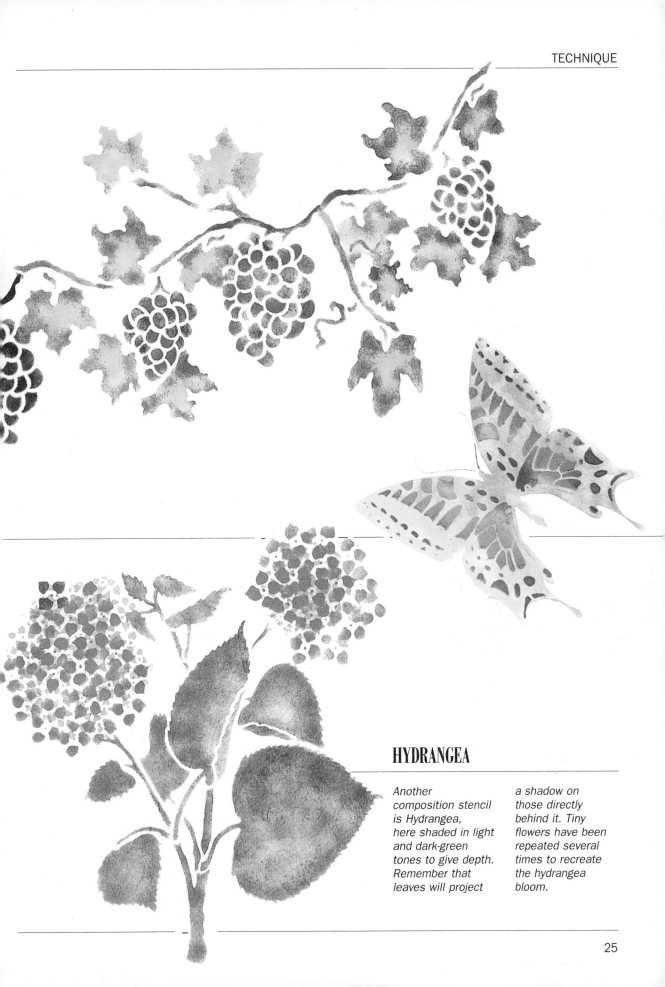

HYDRANGEA

Another composition stencil is Hydrangea, here shaded in light and dark-green tones to give depth. Remember that leaves will project a shadow on those directly behind it. Tiny flowers have been repeated several times to recreate the hydrangea bloom.

STENCIL DESIGNS YOU CAN CUT YOURSELF

With a cutter, some acetate or plastic film and a little imagination you can create your own repertory of stencils. Below are some of the more popular designs, complete with the necessary bridges. In each example, cut just one motif and then give vent to your flair for composition.

Cut a house, a tree and a snowman, then place one house behind the other and the trees around in groups.

The boats sail
in groups;
use this stencil as a
border, changing
the position of
the boats to create
movement.

The geese
could be made
to look in
alternating
directions.

The rosebuds climb
like a real plant;
just keep turning
your stencil to vary
the design and
pattern.

A sense of
movement can
be given to
this motif by
spacing the
swans with a
heart.

COMPOSITION

A climbing plant, a grape vine, a bouquet of flowers, ivy or wisteria are all ideal composition subjects.

Composition stencils are very often composed of three to four elements. A bouquet of flowers can be divided into three parts: the vase, the flowers and a spray of leaves. The leaves and flowers are then composed to make them appear to grow out of the vase.

If you are stencilling wisteria or a climbing rose, start with the part that gives form to the composition – the branches for instance – then when your plant has an artistic direction, start placing the flowers and leaves.

ROSE AND TRELLIS

A climbing rose is an easy subject for beginners. Shade the vase darker at the outer edges, leaving a lighter area towards the centre; this effect creates volume.

FRUIT AND VEGETABLE BORDER

This border should not be too repetitive. Change the order of subjects to create a different pattern, varying the border every now and then.

COLOUR COMBINATIONS

Not everyone is born with a keen sense of colour. Some people possess a natural flair for chromatic combinations, while others find themselves choosing shades and hues without any particular orientation. The best way to appreciate colours is to become more acquainted with them, and it is useful to observe and note down pleasing colour combinations. Similarly, you should take note of your dislikes, and learn to be critical. By this method you develop tastes and preferences – the first steps to working constructively with colour.

PRIMARY COLOURS

Red, blue and yellow are the primary colours. Primary in this case means the origin or source of all known tints and hues. Some artists only carry with them the three primary colours, plus black and white. But mixing tones can be a laborious process, since many colours are obtained with one primary and two secondary, or two secondary and one tertiary, and so on. It is preferable to have a good choice of ready-mixed tints at your disposal.

SECONDARY AND TERTIARY COLOURS

The secondary colours are obtained by mixing together two primary colours: red and yellow make orange; blue and yellow make green; red and blue make violet. These secondary hues complete the colour wheel, but the more interesting ones are to be

found among the tertiary colours, which are obtained by mixing a primary with a secondary or a primary with two secondaries: blue and green make turquoise; red, orange and violet make porpora.

It is a good idea to experiment with colours and invent personal recipes for tints you wish to repeat in future decorations.

COMPLEMENTARY COLOURS

When we look at the colour wheel we see the primary colours and their component secondaries; we can also see at a glance which colours complement each other. Complementary colours are situated directly opposite their correspondent on the wheel. Secondary green is the complement of primary red. Orange is correspondent to violet, and so on. This is the characteristic of a complementary colour: it visually balances its correspondent. To test this correspondence, stare at a colour for at least ten seconds, then look at a white sheet of paper. The original colour's correspondent appears on the white surface.

When combining colours into interesting hues and tints, we need to "perceive" the component colours within a given shade; this enables us to repeat the recipe and supplies a ready mix-and-match selection of coordinating colours.

NEUTRALS

In the case of many interior decoration schemes, an assortment of colours has been interwoven in the various elements of which the scene is composed. Consequently, the introduction of other hues of definite colour could upset the careful chromatic balance. In this case we can use a series of neutral tones not easily definable at pigment level. Neutral tints are obtained by mixing a small quantity of a given colour with white paint. Should you wish to use more than one neutral tone, offset the balance by combining one darker tone with two lighter ones, or vice versa.

When using neutrals there is no risk of one dominating the others; they will all blend equally. For a uniform effect, neutral tones are always composed of a large amount of white and a small quantity of pigment colour.

COLOUR VALUES

The term "tone" refers to the intensity or value of a given colour. Certain colours are therefore described as being "lighter" or "darker" than others. Tones become particularly relevant when three colours are combined in a frieze. A three-colour scheme must be composed of hues with the same tonal value, otherwise the elements in a stronger tone will tend to stand out, vying with the others, and hence unbalance the border.

ROPE AND RING

Cordella is a rope stencil knotted into a ring. With all the semblance of a rope trimming, Cordella offers a pretty motif for "hanging" a painting or print. An even balance of two to three colours is essential for this stencil.

SHADING

What would paintings be without shading, without light and dark tones to suggest volume? The three-dimensional illusion that we so often add to still-life objects is sometimes only the trick of a brushstroke.

We have already seen that a stencil brush is flexible and has a head of long, soft bristles tightly packed together. Using a steady rotary movement, we can put more or less pressure on the brush. More pressure produces a stronger tone, less pressure a lighter tone. For the very best results, always wipe your brush two or three times on absorbent paper after dipping the tip of the bristles in the paint. Never clean your brush with water during the painting operation, nor dilute your paints with water.

TONAL VALUES

The tonal value of a colour must always be taken into consideration when working with a tone-on-tone shading scheme.

A foolproof way of preparing a three-tone scheme is to dose a small amount of the key colour into three different plates, adding white to one, a small amount of black to another, and keeping the third one unchanged; this serves as the intermediate tone.

BALUSTRADE

These columns are a good example of how shading can transform a flat surface into a rounded one. First decide where the light is coming from; the edge on the far side from the light will be the darkest point, the edge nearest to the light less dark, while the bulging part nearest to the observer will be the lightest of all. The colours to use here are natural raw sienna, lampblack and zinc white. Mix the first two in equal parts, adding only a small quantity of black. Start by stencilling the edges first, then work towards the centre of the column with rotating, fluid strokes. Build up the colour around the edges, gradually pushing down on your brush for a stronger tone.

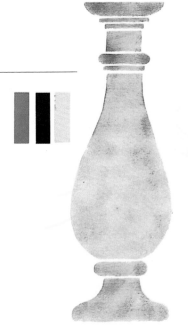

BUTTERFLY

This butterfly is rather a challenging stencil but very satisfying for those who have some prior experience in shading.
One overlay is used for the background of the wings, the other for the characteristic markings.

Use very little paint for the background colour, then give the outside part of the wings a stronger tone by putting more pressure on the brush.

Continue the colour over the central part of the wings, then position the second overlay.

For good results use a strong colour for the outer part of the wings where shading is darker, and pastel colours on the inside portion.

MULBERRY

Mulberry is composed of a delicate leaf motif arranged in sequence to give a twining movement.

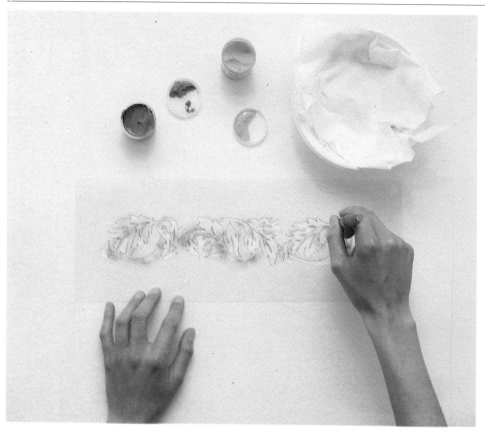

Use tone-on-tone colours, starting with the palest.

Stencil areas here and there, leaving portions white.

Now use a darker tone to fill in the white areas by putting more pressure on the brush.

CORDELLA

Try this cord stencil. The ropes hang one over the other; the nearest cord to us will be darker and more well-defined. The one behind will be lighter and appear to fade into the background.

ROWS OF BOWS

Bows should be shaded to give the effect of the folds where the ribbon turns. Shading will also simulate the satin texture of the bow.

BIG BOW

Likewise, big bow has a look of satin ribbon; use light and dark shading.

CUSHION BOW

Here is a perfect bow for a cushion. The ribbon corner device nicely frames the cushion. Give a darker tone to indicate a twist where the ribbon turns. Likewise, shade the inside of the bow at least three times darker than the outside, leaving points of light on the rounded part.

SPATA

A popular vase for flower arrangements is Spata. Its decorative mouldings have been shaded to make each one stand out separately and simulate a bas-relief. Start by shading the edge mouldings, leaving only the barest amount of paint along the centre. The curved outer sections are darker and more pronounced to accentuate the shape of the vase.

PALLADIO

As its name suggests, Palladio is a neoclassical vase shaped like a cup. The sense of volume can only be obtained by careful shading. Dark shadows appear on the under lip, melting away along the centre, but continuing down the sides. The base of the cup is again given a darker shade: lighter on the protruding ring, and again darker where the stem thins.

The joining element, at the place where the stem is thinnest, must be dark in order to offset the rounded relief of the handle surface, with its clearer, "sfumato" tones. The colours of the Palladio stencil are white, natural sienna, and Vandyke brown. The first two should be applied in equal quantities, to which a touch of Vandyke brown may be added.

ALADDIN

Aladdin has the typical, rounded curve of an oriental vase. Here the light shines left to right, so increase shading on the right, leaving a white patch for the bulge.

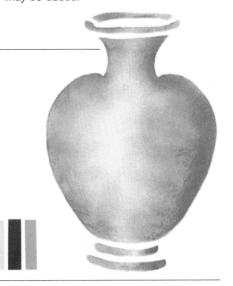

ROSS

This Renaissance frieze is a variation of the classical vine. Stencilled in two tones – dark blue and light blue – its fluid movement is accentuated by the darker coloured elements that rise and fall in an undulating movement.

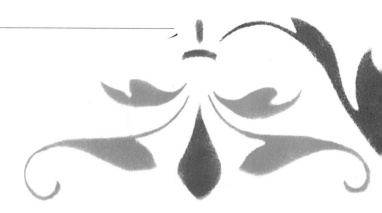

ROMAN VINE

The Roman vine is less ornamental than its Gothic counterpart. Here the small undulating movement has been accentuated by shading the tips of the leaves in a contrasting colour.

TUNISIA

This simple but decorative border of arabesque origin comes alive in two contrasting colours. First stencil the outer "coronets" in green, leaving the centre white, then using brick red, colour the centre portion moving out towards the green coronets. Lastly use the flame-red tone to stencil the small flower motif. Tunisia can be coordinated with geometric stencils or integrated into a scheme with kilim patterns or ethnic designs.

GOTHIC VINE

The Gothic vine can be coloured in shades. Start by stencilling the elements that give movement to the border in a predominant shade.

Stencil the outer edges of the leaves, using a lighter colour for contrast. Gently extend the colour from the border inwards, encroaching

on the main colour. To give further movement, turn your stencil round and link with the previous leaf to create a diagonal where the two repeats join.

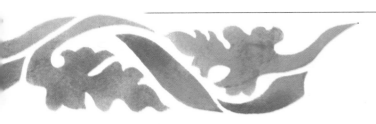

GOTHIC BORDER

This gothic border twists and turns. It is shaded darker on the more pronounced

underside, and lighter where the vine turns above, creating a rhythmic, twisting pattern.

AMENDOLA AND CLEOPATRA

The Amendola and
Cleopatra designs (above
and below) bear the
typical palm-leaf and lotus-
flower emblem of Egypt.

Shade the palms from
dark at the base to light
at the edges. Use tone-on-
tone colour combinations.
The various mobile parts,

especially in Amendola,
make it essential to stick
the stencil firmly to the
surface to avoid
smudging.

OAK LEAF

This border needs tonal
shading to bring the
leaves to life.
Start by applying the
lightest colours:

first yellow, then use
oxide green and
raw sienna
to complete the effect;
stencil the leaves

darker in some places,
lighter in others.
Finish the small
border in
burnt sienna.

ROSE OF PEACE

These roses are shaded slightly darker in the folds of the petals and at the centre, and lighter where the petal turns. Use a chrome yellow green for the leaves and magenta primary for the roses and bud.

TULIPS OF AMSTERDAM

A bed of tulips growing side-by-side provides a certain depth of field. Start with yellow, giving a base shade to all the leaves; then with a stronger green give contrasts of light and dark. The tulips are first stencilled yellow then dabbed over in brick red.

FLORAL MOTIFS

Flower stencils are much more convincing if they are converted from real flower drawings. These flowers were first drawn by hand and then transferred to stencils (see p. 14). Use flower pictures as a guide to shading leaves and petals.

Flower stencils can be framed with a sponged passe-partout (see sponging techniques p. 48, and passe-partout p. 134 for a colourful and unusual flower print).

TROMPE-L'ŒIL EFFECT

An easy way of obtaining a trompe-l'oeil effect is with a teapot, cups, plates and a coffee pot. The illusion occurs when objects are placed on different planes and appear to stand one behind the other. Here space is created by the cups and teapot placed in the foreground, while the plates are seen on the plane behind.

Before you start, decide which objects will be in the foreground and which placed behind. Those nearest will be darker and more distinct, while those behind will be a little lighter and less clearly outlined. Remember that objects in the foreground will be their natural size, but those placed far behind could be considerably smaller.

First stencil the cups nearest to you, then create one cup behind these by placing the stencil over the cup in the foreground and masking the portion which would not be seen. Make the edge that separates the two cups a little darker and defined to "lift" one cup off the other. The object behind should be slightly higher and just a shade lighter. Repeat the same process with the teapot and plates. Lightly shade the inside portion of the plate to indicate an inside curve.

SPONGING AND RAGGING

We use sponging to create depth and give a cloudy light-and-dark effect to walls or furniture. A stencil on a sponged background may seem to "float" over the surface, detaching itself from the background. This so-called special effect is obtained with a natural sponge lightly tinted with acrylic or poster paint.

Put a small amount of paint into a saucer and mix with a little water; the substance should be creamy. Paint the points of the sponge with the colour and dab it over the surface turning your sponge often to avoid repeating the same pattern. Do not put too much pressure on the sponge or the effect will be blotchy and uneven.

For a tone-on-tone look, start with the lightest shade and build up the colour gradually ending with the strongest tone. Ragging will produce a larger imprint. The ragged effect is obtained by the use of a cloth crumpled up into small folds. Any cotton rag will do, but make sure you have enough of the same kind to finish the job. Using the same paints as for sponging, add a small amount of gel and mix well together. The gelatinous mixture thus obtained has a translucent quality and will slip and slide just as oil paints do. Apply the gel thinly to the surface and dab the crumpled cloth over the paint, twisting and turning your rag frequently to create an even imprint.

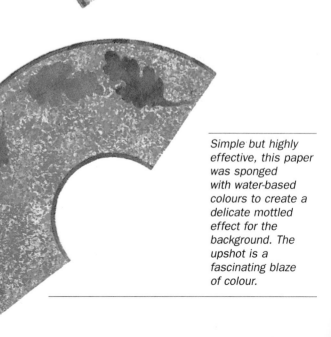

Simple but highly effective, this paper was sponged with water-based colours to create a delicate mottled effect for the background. The upshot is a fascinating blaze of colour.

Three "textures" of slightly different consistency, one prepared with water-based colours, and two with oil-based. They are very effective with their tone-on-tone colouring.

This corner peony pattern has been stencilled onto a sponged apricot background, giving a slightly three-dimensional effect. The flowers seem to float across the surface.

IDEAS

GIFT WRAPPING PAPER

Stencilling is very successful on paper, as seen here on gift wrapping. Choose a paper that has an opaque finish and is not too delicate. If the paper is of a dark colour you can first stencil your design in white and then go over it in your chosen colours. If you prefer a pastel shade as a background, then use strong bold tints to make a colourful contrast. As an alternative you can always sponge your wrapping paper first and then stencil over in matching tones.

This pale blue paper offers a perfect setting for these multicoloured tropical fish. Fish 'n' Shells on p. 109 is an appealing stencil for a bathroom or child's room.

We chose Peony Corner, an elegant flower motif for this pale blue wrapping. As paper is highly absorbent, it responds well to water-based colours. Several shades can be applied by using very little paint and superimposing the tones one over the other.

BLACK AND GOLD

This elegant Christmas motif can easily be rendered with an arabesque border pattern, to great effect. If your black wrapping paper is shiny you can use ceramic gold paint. Shake the bottle well to mix the gold powder with the paint. We used black hard-surface paint for the gold paper. It is advisable to wait 10-15 minutes before each application.

GILDED EFFECT

To create this highly contrasting effect, the black box was gilded with gold leaf, using a stencil as a template. The surface was sprayed with adhesive spray first, then the gold leaf was placed over the stencil and gently dabbed with a stencil brush until completely free of the stencil.

STENCILLING ON FURNITURE

Furniture can be made to look new with a coat of paint, broken-colour techniques, or a stencilled border. The pieces most commonly given this face-lift are cupboard doors, tables, chests of drawers, chairs and seats.

The method used to treat furniture varies considerably according to the surface in question. If you are painting old furniture, it is a good idea to clean the surface well with paint cleaner or spirit.

Use wood primer as an undercoat if the surface is to be painted. If you are stencilling directly onto the wood without a base coat, the wood should be completely free of cleaning polish or furniture wax.

If you are stencilling on natural wood, no preparation is necessary.

Alkyd gel can be used with the special alkyd paints to give a natural, gentle colour base to furniture. Alkyd paints do not require an undercoat or protective varnish, since they are completely waterproof.

COLOURWASHING

To colourwash you can either use poster paints in the creamy version or the powder type.

The paint or powder should be mixed with water until well diluted. Colourwashing works best on natural wood, that is, wood in its completely natural state (without wood-stainer or varnish). If the wood has a striking grain, it will show through the colour.

Using a wide brush, apply the watery mixture to the surface, making the effect as streaky as possible; then, without waiting, proceed to rub the colour well into the surface with a wet cloth. Next, using a dry cloth amalgamate the colour and absorb some of the liquid.

At this point more colour is added, directly from the pot. Streak the paint over the surface, moving in the same direction as the grain. Now rub with a wet cloth. Lastly, protect the surface with an oil-based varnish.

To decorate this chest of drawers we have used an undiluted white acrylic paint, pasted directly onto the surface to obtain the colourwashed look.

EVENING STAR

A stencilled border on a chair can be matched perfectly with existing decorations, as seen here. The tones in the stencil have been coordinated with the bright flowered curtain; the stencil was then repeated on the wall.

TUNISIA
FOR A PALE PINK DESK

This desk was painted with alkyd gel and paints; the border was then stencilled using quick-drying ceramic colours. No top varnish was needed, as alkyd paints have a lacquer quality when dry.

BREAKFAST ON THE TERRACE

A pleasant way to start the morning would be a quiet breakfast on a sunny balcony. These deck chairs are equally at home on the terrace in town and on board a yacht. The stencil we selected, Cordella, a rope and knot design, works excellently in both settings. Put pressure on the brush when stencilling the heavy canvas weave, so as to obtain a darker imprint. Shading is difficult on canvas, so just concentrate on a single, strong colour.

OLD DOOR WITH FLOWERS

This door originally had glass panelling. We replaced the panes with wood and gave it a coat of ivory emulsion paint. The bouquets of flowers: orchids, irises, liliums and lilies were originally drawn to be arranged in vases, but here they make a striking central motif on their own.

FRUIT FOR A KITCHEN CUPBOARD

Fruit motifs give these kitchen cupboards a colourful face-lift. Depending on the surface of the cupboard (it is advisable to try out your paints first), you will decide whether to use acrylics or the more adherent ceramic paints. Kitchen cupboards are often laminated for easy cleaning; in this case, ceramic waterproof paints are preferable.

TABLE AND FLOOR TO MATCH

This sofa table was first painted a yellow green with water-based emulsion paint, then sponged over in sea green and yellow cadmium poster paints diluted in a little water. Peony Corner, a flower motif was encircled round the table top and repeated as a corner motif on the floor. The natural wood floor required a thin coat of colour in pale yellow green, as for the base of table. When colourwashing wood floors, use large brushes and a watery solution of paint. Very soon after the colour has been applied, start rubbing the paint into the surface.

Next, using a dry cloth to absorb excess liquid, continue rubbing the colour in the same direction as the wood grain. When dry, the colour will be at least two shades lighter than the one originally used.

HOW TO GIVE HOUSEHOLD OBJECTS A NEW LOOK

With a discerning eye and some flair for colour and design, you can transform any plain or uninteresting household object into a characteristic and highly personalised article. Objects that are easy to start with include ceramic vases, photo frames, lampshades, wooden boxes, place mats, hat boxes, cushions, table mats and other such household items. When you have gained confidence with these small objects you will certainly wish to try your hand at more creative ventures, such as friezes and wall compositions. When choosing motifs for wall borders, the colours and designs should match up well with existing decorations.

You can obtain clues and ideas from your curtains or sofa cover fabrics. Patterns on cloth often provide excellent ideas for matching stencils to upholstery or to window treatments.

ROSE BORDER

Roses are always a favourite when it comes to interior decoration. This rose border can also be transformed into a climbing rose by positioning the roses and leaves to form a ramage, just as the natural plant would grow.

RADIATOR COVER DECORATED WITH ROSES

Radiators are a thorn in the side of interior decorators. These unattractive but essential pieces of equipment tend to be placed under windows, along corridors, in alcoves and in just about any other place where pipes are easily reached. We have devised a clever way of camouflaging the radiator. A screen in medium-density fibreboard covers the front of the radiator. The background was sponged with alkyd paints and stencilled in hard-surface acrylics. I advise using a composition wood, such as chipboard or MDF, since these do not bend or buckle when exposed to heat.

PHOTO COMPOSITION

Photograph compositions using portraits offer a novel way to personalise a corner wall of your bedroom. You will need photos of more or less the same size and type (portraits or family groups), a white cardboard sheet, poster paints for sponging, and our Ring Bow stencil. The central photo should be a striking picture that catches the eye; the others should then be symmetrically arranged around it. Cut out different geometric shapes in the cardboard passepartout, varying them from round to oval, octagonal and rectangular. Arrange them in pairs. Sponge the cardboard in a delicate pastel shade to offset the dark photos. Over each photo stencil the Ring Bow giving it darker shades of colour in the folds of the ribbon. When possible let the two ends of the bow hang down under the photo. The pictures should look as if they are suspended by the bow. With a felt-tip pen of the same colour as the bows trace the contours of each "window" with a thin border to finish the edge. Insert the photos behind the windows and paint the frame in the same colour as the bows.

RING BOW

Ring Bow is a decorative stencil useful for hanging pictures or photos. Apart from the composition opposite, the bows can also be used to hang paintings or prints or be used on their own as a pretty border.

DECORATIVE HATBOXES

Hatboxes have more uses than one. They may contain a hat, but more often they are wonderful storage spaces for all sorts of small items that have no fixed place: scarves, ribbons, cassettes, photos, jewellery, and so forth. When covered with wallpaper, the surface of these boxes become ideal for stencilling. A final coat of protective varnish makes them more resistant to knocks and tears.

Using acrylic colours for hard surfaces, paint a wide border around the lid. Select a design that repeats well around the box and stencil it in the same colour as the border.
Paper tends to mark easily, so a coat of water-based varnish should be applied over the whole surface.
Like bows linked together, Rows of Bows form a rhythmic pattern round this hatbox.

CHINESE VASE PLACE MATS

Characteristic and decorative, Chinese vases are fun to stencil and make excellent central motifs on cupboard doors and wall compositions, or on objects such as these place mats. Since the design on the vase is quite intricate, be sure to stick the stencil well with adhesive tape so that all the mobile parts adhere to the surface while stencilling.

The bases for place mats are made of MDF and measure approximately 30 x 25 cm. The corners have been cut diagonally to give a less square shape to the mat. Start by painting the surface white with an oil-based emulsion.

SPONGING

Put a small quantity of alkyd gel in a saucer and mix with liquid ceramic paints. Paint the points of the sponge with the creamy mixture.

Starting with the lighter blue tone, sponge the surface with a dabbing movement.

Without waiting for the first coat to dry, sponge over the darker blue tone.

Allow to dry, then stencil the vase using hard-surface paints; finish with an oil-based varnish to protect the design and give brilliance to the colour.

TABLECLOTHS

CLASSIC BORDER CALLED ROSS

Of part-Classical part-Gothic inspiration, Ross has the movement of a vine spreading and twisting its leaves. Here on this elegant tablecloth in stark black and white it forms a rhythmic pattern, neatly intersecting at the corner. Use Ross for a curtain border, or wall frieze at skirting level or below the ceiling. For these designs, only cloth paints were used.

GREEK KEY

Always a classic favourite, the Greek key is easily converted into a stencil. We choose a white background once again to offset the striking contours of the design. A little care is needed in planning the repeats; if the key is used as a frame very rarely can one obtain a perfect 90° angle, so plan your border to fill the corner in order not to finish in a half-motif. Use fabric paint only when stencilling cloth; synthetic fibres are not ideal for painting since they do not absorb the paint. For the very best results use 100% cotton fabric. To fix fabric colours, wait for at least 12 hours then iron with a hot iron on the right side of the design; machine wash as for delicates.

CANDLE SHADES

Small shades atop "marbled" candle-stands are becoming popular decorative items for mantelpieces, bookcases, shelves and wall brackets. All you need to make them is some extra wallpaper left over from your last decorating project. Plain colours or marbled backgrounds work best for light reflection.

STRAWBERRY HILL

Spiky leaves spaced with a little flower make a pretty border for these card lampshades.

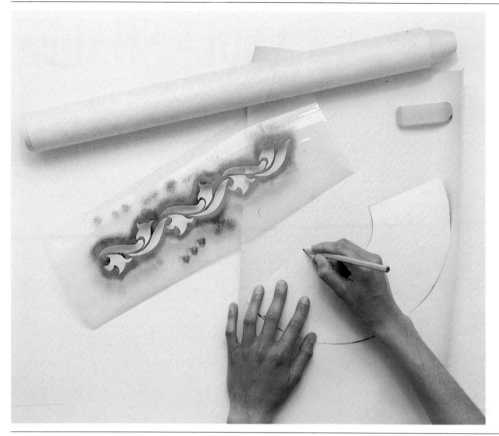

To make your own shades out of leftover wallpaper, take a strip of around 30 cm. A pink to reddish colour will reflect a warm glow; better not to use colours such as green or blue. Using a cardboard template, draw the outline of the shade onto the reverse side of the wallpaper.

Cut around the form as shown in the picture.

A simple stencil
that moves around
the curved shape of
the shade is ideal.
Stencil your border
with hard-surface
acrylic paints.

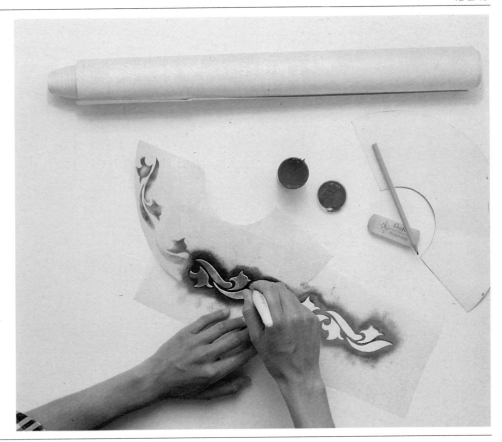

With a felt-tip pen,
draw a thick border
around the top and
bottom of the
shade. Now stick
the two sides
together with water-
based glue. Check
your template for a
perfect half-sphere;
if measurements
are not precise the
two edges will not
join equally.

PLEATED LAMPSHADE

Extra rolls of wallpaper can be used to create a variety of household accessories, from covered boxes to wastepaper baskets, hatboxes and even lampshades.

Wallpaper is an excellent base for stencil paints; it is totally porous and can take any amount of shading. Shown opposite is an example of a pleated lampshade fashioned out of wallpaper, and stencilled with a matching border repeated on the wall behind. To make this pretty shade you will need a piece of wallpaper 30 cm long, biasbinding in a contrasting colour, satin ribbon, water-based glue, and a clipper for punching holes. Where possible choose a light-coloured wallpaper with a plain background.

Cut a length of paper 30 cm long and stencil your Orefici border.

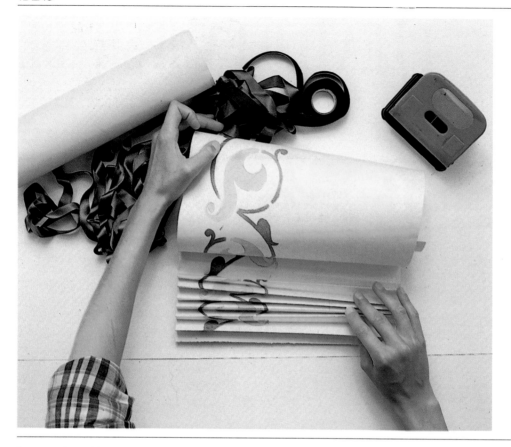

Make concertina pleats by folding the paper back and forth into 2 cm folds. Take care to pleat each fold to exactly the same measurement and continue until all 30 cm are pleated.

Using an adhesive stick, glue the biasbinding to the top and bottom of the shade.

Make small holes
on the inside
of each pleat.

Now thread the
satin ribbon through
the holes and
tighten up the
pleats. Glue the
edges of the
shade together.

NEEDLEWORK CUSHION

A stencil can also be used as a pattern for needlework or needlepoint cushions, tablecloths, etc. Use fabric stencil paints when stencilling the canvas. It is a good idea to use strong, bold colours, as the design is seen through the holes of the canvas and tends to loose those shapes in delicate colours. Shading leaves and flowers will be important to the final contrasted light-and-dark composition. Start with pale tones and build up the contrast with the stronger colours in places where leaves and flowers are shadowed.

DECORATED BOXES FOR JEWELLERY

Small boxes for storing all sorts of items from jewellery to visiting cards are always useful on a desk or dressing table. These boxes come in natural wood. They were first painted with acrylic colours diluted in a little water and then lightly sponged. For the stencils on both boxes colours were mixed that would blend into the background. Use an oil-based colourless varnish to protect the surface. If you wish to antique the box, gently sandpaper the edges and corners of the lid to give it a worn look, then rub a wood stainer over the sandpapered corners.

TERRACOTTA POTS

Terracotta and clay are ideal materials for stencilling. Their earthenware quality has a rustic uneven surface that is highly porous. Should you have some old terracotta pots in the garden, put these in the sun to dry for a few days. Earthenware retains humidity and it is this damp surface that dilutes the paint and ruins the stencilling design. If the sun does not do the trick, you can always put the pots in the oven for about half an hour. When thoroughly dry, paint the pots a bright, sunny colour – any water-based paint will do – but keep the mixture thick. Terracotta needs a solid coat of paint to over its reddish-brown colour.

If the chosen base colour does not cover the dark terracotta sufficiently, then paint the base white first, then apply your overall colour. Owing to the rough surface of the pots, the outline of your stencil will not be perfect.

The result however, is a pleasing rustic composition well-suited to country settings or on window sills or in groups of decorative vases bunched together. To combat humidity, varnish your pots with a strong boat varnish; this will completely seal the surface.

The Almeria grape-vine stencil lends a naïf quality to this fruit bowl painted in canary yellow, earth green and primary red. When selecting colours for pots, try a bold contrast between base coat and motif, thus when your pots are in bloom the resulting explosion of colour makes an attractive shelf décor, or a striking window box.

COLOURWASHED WOODEN TRAY

Natural wood is preferable to wood that has been varnished. A colourful technique can be achieved on natural wood using poster or acrylic paints diluted in water; the grain of the wood "shines through" the muted colours and appears in lighter and darker streaks across the surface. We painted the ground in cadmium orange and stencilled bright yellow lemons as a corner motif.

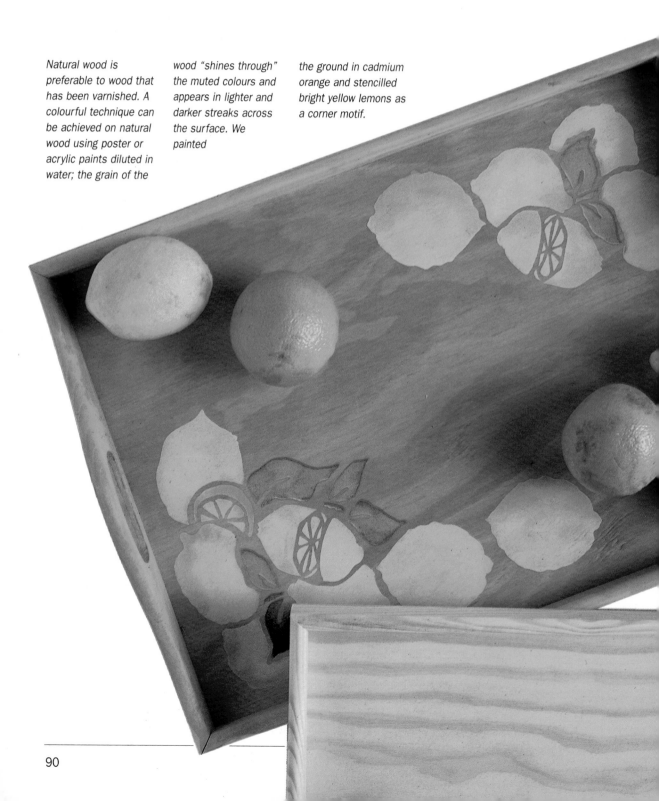

Poster paint has been diluted in water to a thin consistency. The mixture is then streaked over the surface, leaving some areas free of paint. Without waiting, rub the colour into the wood, putting more pressure in some areas than in others. Using a dry cloth rework the surface, soaking up any excess liquid. For an antiqued effect use white undiluted paint, streaking it over the surface in the direction of the wood grain and then rub with a dry cloth.

Leave your work to dry, then proceed with the stencilling using ceramic paints. These will give the surface a nice shiny look, instead of the opaque effect of hard-surface paints.

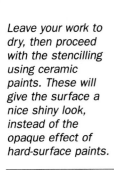

PANSIES
FOR A GREEN TRAY

This natural wood tray was given a coat of wood primer before painting it with oil-based emulsion. We used ceramic paints to stencil the pansies on the shiny emulsion surface. Shading effects can be achieved with ceramic paints by dabbing one colour over the other after an interval of 10 to 20 minutes. This gives time for the previous application to become "tacky" and accept the paint without mixing. Use a strong boat varnish as a final protective coat.

COORDINATING FABRIC DESIGNS WITH A STENCIL

As previously mentioned many decorating fabrics supply us with ready inspiration for motifs and ramage to be used as wall stencils. This unusual fabric of green-grey vines with tints of terracotta was the inspiration behind the grape composition used for this wall. You will not easily find shades such as these in the range of colours available for stencilling, so try out your skills at mixing paints; if you do not get it right a first, keep trying various combinations until one works. To give a rustic look to your grapevine, try two or three harmonising tones, dabbing one over the other until you obtain a blotchy texture.

Sometimes you come across a lucky match, as in the case of this handsome material and our grape-vine stencil.

CURTAINS, CUSHIONS AND BORDERS

Coordinating friezes with existing decorations or creating accessories that mix and match with stencil borders, has long been a pleasant challenge for interior decorators. Opposite we used a Gothic vine stencil to create a coordinated range of items comprising a curtain border, a cushion cover and a wallpaper frieze. A roll of extra wallpaper can be cut into strips and used as a base for the stencilled border.

We used a heavy natural cotton fabric for the curtain, as natural fibres accept fabric paint well; just iron on the right side with a hot steam iron to fix the colour and machine wash as for delicates.

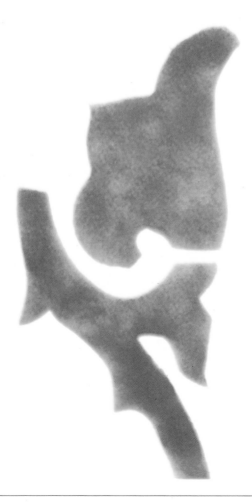

BED SHEETS AND PILLOW CASE

Love Knot is a tied bow which can be used vertically or horizontally. If used as a horizontal border, each bow becomes a motif on its own; if used vertically, the ribbons join together to form a succession of bows. If you are painting a lampshade, it should be in natural cotton. The flexibility of your stencil film will allow you to bend it around the shade. Make sure all parts adhere perfectly so as to avoid smudging round the edges.

CLEMATIS, A BORDER FOR A ROLLER BLIND

Clematis is a wide border of leaves and flowers growing chaotically side by side. We needed a conspicuous motif to fill up the large space on this pale pink blind. The blind fabric is a resinated cotton that can be stencilled with fabric or with hard-surface paints. When confronted with a border that forms a frame, the four corners could be a problem if you use a geometric or repetitive pattern. It is always a good idea to start in the middle and work towards the corners. Stencil one motif to the right and one motif to the left of the centre. Stop just short of the corner and proceed to decorate the next side, starting once again in the middle. When you reach the corner find the elements within the design that will join the border harmoniously together. Use a steam iron to fix the colours onto the fabric. If the blind is made of resinated cotton, use hard-surface paints, and then proceed with the ironing.

CERAMICS AND TILES

A new door is opened to those who can master the technique of stencilling on tiles and ceramics. The secrets lie in dosing the paint just to the right consistency on the first application, waiting until this becomes "tacky" and then proceeding to apply layer over layer of paint, building up the thickness and gripping power. Ceramic liquid paints are not fired in an oven, although they can be put in a cool domestic oven for no more than 20 minutes to solidify. Depending on the brand used, most ceramic paints contain a "gripping" ingredient which helps it adhere to the shiny surface. However, it is rather the building up of paint as previously explained that produces the best gripping results. When stencilling tiles, first clean the surface with spirit; then spray the reverse side of the stencil with adhesive spray. Do not spray the tile, as the glue in the spray will leave a sticky film, which is difficult to clean. Place your stencil firmly down on the tile. Put the smallest amount of paint on the brush and wipe it on kitchen paper to remove the excess. Then repeat the process two or three times.

FLEUR-DE-LYS

A pretty toile-de-Jouy fabric offsets these tiles painted in gold ceramic paints. The fleur-de-lys, another revival often chosen for its classical elegance, can be used as a single motif or as an effective rhythmic border. Try alternating the fleur with a geometric form such as the rhomboid contained in the lower part of the stencil.

OLYMPIA

Blue and gold are striking colours for a unique motif recalling the antique palm symbol. Used here on bathroom tiles. An interesting pattern could be obtained by stencilling Olympia on alternate tiles, one veering to the right, the next to the left, or one up and one down, facing first left and then right. For extra protection, apply a coat of colourless varnish over the surface of the tiles.

Wipe the tile well with spirit cleaner to remove any dust or grease; spray the reverse side of the stencil with adhesive spray and press down firmly on the tile.

Using ceramic liquid paints, take up a small amount of paint on the tip of the bristles, wipe them on kitchen paper to absorb some of the liquid. Holding the brush perpendicular to the surface, apply the paint using a dabbing movement.

Wait for at least 7 to 10 minutes until the paint is sticky and nearly dry, then repeat the operation two or three times. This building up of the colour gradually ensures that the paint grips the surface. Remove the stencil with care and allow the paint to dry for at least 12 hours. If you have slightly smudged the paint in places you can clean the area with a cotton swab and spirit.

When the paint is completely dry apply a thick coat of colourless varnish over the whole surface.

FISH AND SHELLS

A happy marine composition can be devised using these simple motifs of shells and fish. Try giving variation to the pattern, so as to make an attractive border decoration for a bathroom wall.

Shading the fish in different tones can be achieved by laying one colour over the other at intervals of 7 to 10 minutes. Start with the lighter colours first, or at least a shade or two lighter than the tone you intend to use for the shading.
The first coat will become tacky and the second will amalgamate into it. Use a dabbing movement, keeping your brush perpendicular to the surface.

PAVIA

A simple leaf motif called Pavia adorns a collection of white china. A little care was needed when stencilling this curved and elaborate leaf on a shiny rounded surface. We first cleaned the china well with spirit, then the stencil was cropped to free it from the surrounding area. All that was left was a small portion encircling the design. Spray the back of the stencil, lay it over the surface and gently spray again. In this way we apply adhesive spray to the part to be decorated allowing the paint to grip the surface better. Proceed to stencil in the same way as for the tiles.

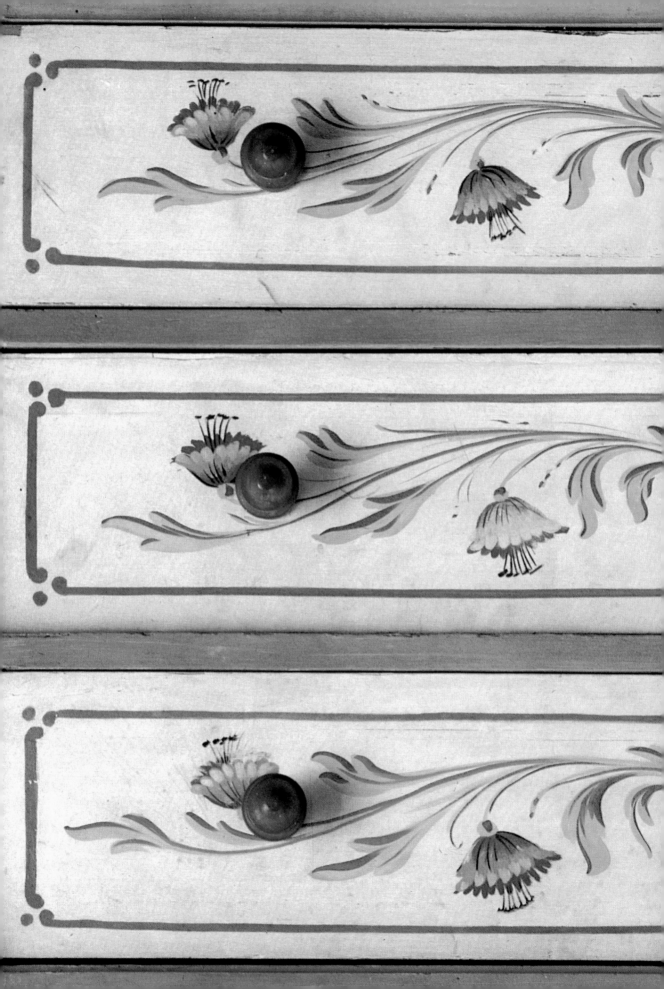

PROJECTS

DECORATION SCHEMES WITH STENCILLING

The universal popularity of stencilling is entirely due to its sheer versatility, to its capacity to be integrated into any interior decoration scheme. Given that a motif can be borrowed from a curtain fabric, a pattern on a carpet, from a porcelain jug or plate, as well as from the design of inlaid wood, and subsequently turned into a stencil, its potential is enormous. Stencils are at home in virtually any setting, be it classical, rustic, or elegant.

INSPIRATION

Friezes, frescoes, and wall decorations in general greatly improve the contours of a boxy room or one with a high ceiling or large expanses of wall. Such rooms usually lack atmosphere. So much can be done, but before you start you should take a close look at the proportions and irregularities of the place you wish to decorate. You may find that a part of the room has an odd shape. If so, you might divide this extra space with a screen, decorating it with stencils. Alternatively, you might create an arch and decorate the inside curve. You may get stuck with electrical wires or water pipes running along a corridor, or down the side of a door. In that case, why not make a panel to cover these and stencil on it a climbing ivy? If ceilings seem too high, a running border set at 30 cm from the top of the wall helps to bring the ceiling nearer. If on the other hand your ceilings are too low, you can decorate a border directly on the ceiling. This optical device gives the impression of height. When you gain sufficient confidence at stencilling, try your hand at panelling. If you already have a dado rail in the form of a cornice, stencil a small border under the rail and then a series of panels, some vertical and some horizontal, to create movement. Of all the reasons for choosing a stencil, perhaps the most important one is the fact that it becomes an expression of one's personality, a manifestation of one's flair for design.

CREATING AN ATMOSPHERE

The creation of an "atmosphere" in a sitting room, bedroom or even an entrance hall, at first causes some confusion as to exactly how this can be obtained or what indeed the term may mean in the field of house decoration. It is indeed an elusive concept, but it is essential to the success of an interior scheme.

When a room has been completed, you may feel that it nonetheless lacks atmosphere. However, the creation of atmosphere at a later stage is a difficult task. Once the lighting is in position, and once the walls are decorated and furnishings chosen and placed, any modification is a trial-and-error process.

Without doubt the most important element that contributes to the atmosphere of a scheme is the light source. Natural light is the most engaging; colours will be seen in their true tones, pale shades will reflect the light, while darker colours will lose some of their saturation and appear more brilliant. If you do not have the fortune to live in a luminous apartment or in the country, where natural light abounds, then you must install an efficient system of artificial lighting to compensate for the lack of natural light. Lighting subjects such as bookcases, paintings, niches, alcoves, corners far from a window, a wall between two windows become important in the task of creating points of interest and accents of light. Task lighting was specially designed for this purpose. Sources of light will illuminate a particular area not otherwise covered by ambient lighting. It is this type of illumination that can radically change a gloomy anonymous room into one where lighting effects generate interest and create atmosphere.

OREFICI

Here the antique vine appears once again in the form of Orefici, seen here in blue and yellow.

When using two contrasting tones, the lighter one will "shine out" and give movement to the

border, as in this representation. The eye follows a pattern of yellow swirls.

115

BEFORE YOU START

Study the room you are about to decorate. How high is the ceiling? Where is the light source? What shape is the room? How many windows are there? Does it face north or south? When you have considered all these details, think of how you can improve the proportions with a frieze or a repetitive motif, such as that of wallpaper or a plant ramage.

CEILINGS TOO HIGH OR TOO LOW

The higher the ceiling, the more the room seems to have vertical emphasis. This problem is often the case in Victorian houses that have been renovated and divided into small flats with very contained spaces. Where ceilings were originally planned for larger rooms, a border just below the ceiling helps "correct" this fault. In the opposite case, a very low ceiling can be greatly improved by placing a small motif in each corner, or creating a border.

RHYTHMIC BORDERS

Rhythm is an important feature of interior decoration schemes. A stencilled border with a particularly repetitive theme causes the eye to skip from one motif to the other in rhythmic succession. This is useful for creating a sense of movement to a particularly static situation. Another solution is to create symmetrical images such as two-by-two motifs, or a single motif alternating with a geometric form or stylised flower.

LONG NARROW SPACES

Corridors, landings, dressing rooms, bathrooms and halls are nearly always secondary spaces in house planning. They are "left over" when all other functions have been allocated. And yet these strips or passages perform essential functions within the household. Decorating these narrow spaces requires some planning. The aim here is to create width and bring the ceiling closer. A piece of furniture along one wall can help to open out the space. Boiserie or panelling along the lower half will also tend to pull the walls out.

A running border 30 cm from the ceiling will tend to make it seem lower.

A trompe-l'oeil scene on one or two walls gives illusory depth and creates a greater sense of space. A word of warning about mirrors: they are a poor solution to the problem of space, and might merely reflect the same scene back into the restricted space.

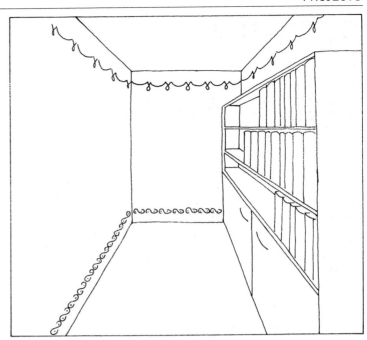

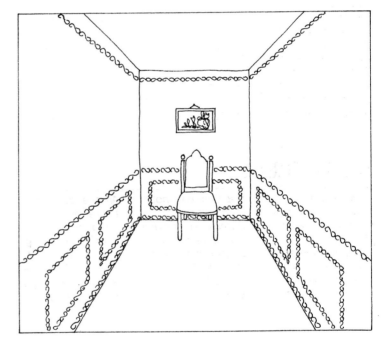

CLASSIC BORDERS
FOR A PRINT-ROOM ALCOVE

For most people, the sitting room is not the first place that comes to mind for stencilling borders. In my experience, few clients or students in the stencilling course actually ventured to paint the walls of their sitting room. They felt that this particular room should be professionally done, or that stencilling is more suitable in a bedroom, bathroom, kitchen or entrance hall. But just take a look at this elegant print-room alcove. The classical lines of old prints and Victorian borders blend wonderfully with the Gothic Vine border, lightly stencilled on the pale-pink, striped wallpaper.

GOTHIC VINE

The print room has recently become a popular decorative theme, and crops up on cupboards, doors, walls and alcoves. Here Gothic Vine mingles perfectly with the print-room alcove. We stencilled it very lightly, to avoid interfering with the strong tones of the classic borders. The motif links together simply by repeating it in the same position, or you can turn the successive motif around to link the leaves up diagonally.

HOW TO MITRE CORNERS

You may wonder how to make a perfect right angle when using a border such as Alhambra. This problem arises whenever you use a geometric pattern, or one of those based on a stylised floral motif. As you can see from the illustration on this page, we have found a solution in which the corner section is designed slightly different from the rest of the border.

Stencil a portion of the border on a strip of paper; you will need at least four complete repeats of the border. This template will make the job much easier. Remember that the more the pattern is geometrical in style, the harder it is to create a proper corner piece.

Photocopy this strip twice. You now have a template to work from. This guide will be used to mitre the corner; it is an indication of the exact position of your stencil in the corner. The two strips of paper must be superimposed at the precise point where the two motifs meet in the corner, one on the lower strip and one on the upper strip.

With a ruler, draw a diagonal line from corner to corner.

Now cut both strips along the diagonal line.

Stick these together with tape and proceed to stencil, following the design exactly. You may need to mask certain parts with tape while completing your corner.

PAINTED CHEST OF DRAWERS

If you ever browse in antique shops, you may be lucky enough to come across a painted chest of drawers, like this one I found in Sicily. The very delicate flower ramage was the inspiration behind the wall stencil used as a frieze. First trace the design on to a piece of paper and see how it could repeat in a border, then organise the various bridges, remembering not to make them too fragile or too wide, as these white spaces tend to break up the design. You can enclose a delicate border within a thin line or very small border; this gives a contour to an indefinite sequence, strengthening its pattern and accentuating its direction.

WALL BRACKET AND A GARLAND OF FLOWERS

This pale sea-green eggshell base is luminous but not too brilliant as a base, and creates an ideal colour for Clematis and Ivy Border. The garland of flowers appears to grow out of the light fitting and fall artistically each side. Stencilling on a coloured background does not present any particular problem, other than the colours you choose. These should first be tried out on the base. They will no longer be seen on a white background, so some chromatic change is inevitable.

SNOWFLAKE WALL STENCIL

Walls in pale cobalt blue could be monotonous and uninteresting without an embellishment such as this snowflake stencil in very pale tones of the same blue. Stencilling on a dark background limits the choice of tones to those of pastel shades that harmonise with the base colour. It is not advisable to use a contrasting colour on a dark background; this makes for too heavy a contrast and overemphasis the wall.

IVY AND HYDRANGEA ARCH

Architecturally speaking arches divide one ambience from another. They mark a transition, but can also be highly decorative if used to their best advantage. Having the sitting room on one side and the library on the other we decided on this creeper and trellis to accent and lend character to the arch. A hydrangea plant with blooms not yet quite open balances the lower region. The leaves of the plant, as those of the ivy are superimposed, an essential technique for creating depth in a composition.

ORANGE TREE FOR A CHILD'S CUPBOARD

A colourful orange tree was chosen for this built-in cupboard framed with an ivy motif. The tree is symmetrically placed dead centre on the two doors and the pot a little way down from the cupboard. The tree is perfectly balanced with the proportions of the cupboard. The oranges can easily be changed to make it a lemon tree.

STENCILLING FLOORS

You will find stencilling floors very gratifying – they are not as difficult to stencil as walls and have twice the decorative impact. You will be rewarded by compliments on your stencilling skill, and more than likely be asked to repeat the excellent work in a friend's house. Do not be put off by large spaces, just organise yourself well. To stencil the "carpet" in this picture, I first taped the area on the outer border and again on the inner border. At this point I had two concentric rectangles. I sponged the wide border, using a marine sponge and acrylic paint diluted in water. Then I painted the inner rectangle a slightly lighter shade and stencilled the orange composition in the middle.

STENCILLING THE CARPET

The "carpet" opposite is stencilled on a painted floor. Not all floors will have a paint finish: many will be untreated, others perhaps stained. If the floor has a wax finish you will need to remove all traces of polish or stainer. Natural wood will take the hard-surface paints better and will not need to be varnished, as the paint seeps into the porous surface. If the wood is painted, then two coats of strong boat varnish are essential to protect and finish the design.

PASTORAL SCENES AND A SINGLE-COLOUR MOTIF

A simple motif decorates the floor and window frame in this bedroom. The Toile-de-Jouy curtain and wall-covering were the main points of interest, so a simple motif stencil was the best choice to coordinate with the busy tableau fabric design. The charming fabric known as Toile-de-Jouy was invented in a small French village of the same name in around 1800. This type of material is generally printed with pictures that describe the life and times of rural France in the nineteenth century. In this picture, the Damask stencil blends perfectly with the Toile-de-Jouy curtains. The floor and woodwork was painted a pale ivory eggshell. Ceramic paints were used for the floor stencil; a coat of colourless varnish was applied to each motif to reinforce the lacquer.

DAMASK

Damask is the name of this stylised flower used for the bedroom opposite. The horizontal rhythmic pattern on the window frame in lacquer red brings out the tableau scenes in the Toile-de-Jouy curtains.

A PRINT-ROOM STENCIL

Here is a rope-and-ring stencil, a novel idea for creating the print-room technique with your brush. Hanging pictures with bows, ropes and ribbons has become a popular ornamental theme in many drawing rooms. The advantage with our stencil version is that you can colour these embellishments to suit your particular colour scheme.

We shaded Cordella in three different hues; sage green, yellow ochre and orange cadmium. They picked out the tones perfectly in the fig print, shown opposite. To complete the colour scheme, we ragged a passe-partout in the same tones.

STENCILLED FRAMES FOR FAMILY PHOTOS

These miniatures are an amusing way of displaying family photos.
So often snaps tend to pile up in boxes or await the right moment to be glued into albums where they are seen on rare occasions. The assortment of close-ups came together while sorting through old photos: first I put aside all the head and shoulder photos, then I picked out a particularly in-focus portrait for the centre motif (always enhance the central part of any composition).
I selected two black-and-white photos of the same size and placed these to the right and left of the centre photo.
The bottom two photos were both taken on the same day at sunset and were of a rich red colour. The top two, smaller than the others, made a perfect pair. This left a vertical photo to position in the middle and slightly above. I chose the bows carefully to match the colours in each photo. Try to vary the size and shape of your frames. An all square or all rectangular ensemble would not be so eye-catching.

Start by drawing a grid of squares 3 x 3 cm, and then trace out the frames to the size you require. If you need to increase the frame size, redraw the grid accordingly.

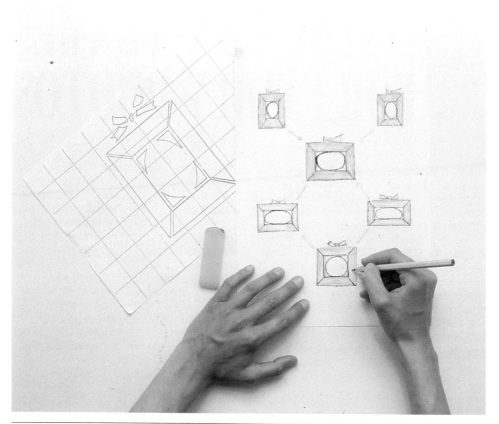

A rough sketch of the placement of the photos helps when measuring up on the wall. The photos are symmetrical two by two, so the pairs should be equidistant from one another and from the nearest photo.

When stencilling the frame give a deeper tone to the corners and along the two edges, leaving the centre portion lighter. The frame will now have a curved effect. Use raw sienna for a light wood frame.

*Place the photo
under the central
oval and
cut around to size.*

*Stick your photo in
the centre using
water-based glue.*

ANTIQUE LOOK

You may have to decorate the walls of an old house or stencil an old piece of furniture. In this case, a sparkling fresh just-painted design would not enhance an old chest of drawers, nor look particularly harmonious on the rough walls of a cottage. Clearly, you need to antique or "rough-up" your handiwork. This may be more challenging than at first appears, and will certainly need a few experiments before you get it right. Always try out your effects first on a similar background to the one you are decorating, to see exactly which method to use and how much of the product is needed. You can antique with crackle glaze. This should be done after carefully reading the instructions, as each product is slightly different. Crackle glaze works by means of a chemical reaction between a water-based product and an oil-based one.

Brush the surface with oil-based glaze mixed with a small amount of raw umber. Sandpaper the area, particularly in places where erosion could occur. Then brush on an antiquing patina to darken the areas just sandpapered. If you prefer, dilute the patina with a colourless mat varnish until you obtain a light brown tone.

POTS OF GERANIUMS

An effective sense of volume was obtained by these pots of geraniums stencilled on a balcony wall. The pot is seen to curve round the back of the plant, helping to create an illusion of depth. Leaves and flowers are seen to superimpose one another.

Use hard-surface acrylics on external walls, as their plastic composition is completely waterproof.

THE DECORATIVE ARTS IN INTERIOR SCHEMES

THREE-DIMENSIONAL MOULDING

A stencil in four overlays magically evolves into a trompe-l'oeil moulding for the ceiling. The light and dark shadows have been scientifically worked out on a computer to correspond to four shades of the same colour: two dark tones, one less intense, a background

Interior decoration has enjoyed a tremendous boom in the last ten years. House-owners have become accustomed to planning decorative schemes and undertaking works such as painting, sponging, stencilling, marbling, and print-room decoupage.

The hobby and leisure time markets have expanded into an industry producing myriad products, all calculated to bring clever techniques and simplified arts within reach.

mid-tone and one very light. Mixing these to perfection is perhaps the most difficult task. You will have to start with the background colour; darken it twice, then lighten it twice. In this way we have a mid-ground tone, plus two slightly darker and two lighter tones.

There are paints that dry in seconds, there are mediums to "move" the paint and make it more malleable. There are agents to mix with oil paints to accelerate the drying process, and there are retarding agents to slow down the quick-drying quality of acrylics.

There are alkyd paints that are oil-based but quick-drying.

There are medium gels to be mixed with paints so they slip and slide, making special effects easier to achieve and produce a more artistic representation.

There are stencils that create a three-dimensional decorative moulding, on which the bridges are afterwards cancelled and the moulding seems to be painted by hand.

These scenographic techniques are now enjoyed and appreciated by countless home-owners wishing to personalise their interiors, using their new-found artistic skills.

TROMPE-L'ŒIL
FOR SLIDING DOORS

The sliding doors in this dining room form a partition with the sitting room. The Chinese cabinet provides an artistic focal point; the doors, therefore, have to be coordinated with the dark green lacquer and black of the Chinese images. Our futuristic composition, not in perfect perspective, has an idealistic charm and a colour scheme in strict harmony with the existing decorations.

TERRACES

This pretty terrace scene was accomplished using trompe-l'oeil and stencilling techniques together. The two techniques of trompe-l'oeil and stencilling are not usually thought of in connection with the same decoration, but this terrace scene was accomplished by combining an adroit use of perspective with a careful selection of stencil patterns. The terracotta tiles and the thin lines continuing off into the distance endow the composition with a strong sense of perspective. The principal pictorial focuses of the design are the balustrade, the pergola, the climbing ivy, and the pots of roses, all carefully designed in proportion on the same plane, and of course all the fruit of stencil work. The

stencils used include a climbing rose and ivy, two classical pots, a trellis (a small portion of trellis will do since you repeat it several times), one balustrade with top rail and base, and clouds of different shapes. Start by dividing your wall into the sections, two-thirds of which will be the sky; of the remaining third make more than half the meadow-green area and the rest, the terrace floor. Start by colouring the sky, darker at the zenith and lighter towards the horizon. The green landscape background has been lent a certain sense of movement by the technique of tone-on-tone sponging with acrylic colours (green, middle green and white), and a classic circular brushing

with the stencil brush in which the lighter tones have been amalgamated with the darker ones.
Colour the fields in different shades of green, giving darker shadows where valleys and woods break up the scene. Take a focal point just below midway down the wall, and draw vanishing lines to the two corners and another one straight down (above).
Divide the two areas created into equal sections with lines departing from your focal point. Place your balustrade slightly down from the focal point (centre). Draw horizontal lines across the floor of the terrace (below).
We now have our tiled floor, rub out alternative horizontal lines to produce a tiled effect.

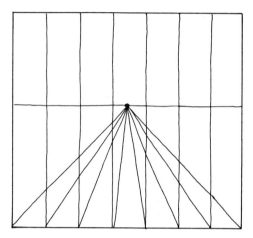

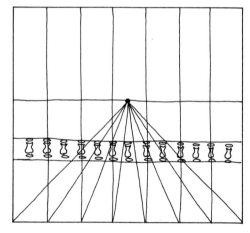

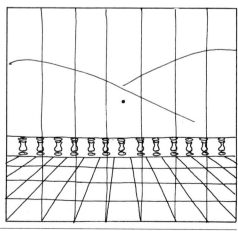

STENCILS
TO COPY

ACKNOWLEDGMENTS

Many thanks are due to Titti, Maria and Allegra of the English Home Design, who helped me enormously till the publication of the book; to Maria Sole Giuliani and Adriana Fossati for the stencils of their own creation; to Rossano Orefici who allowed us to use his classical and Renaissance designs; to Cristina Ugone for her precious advice to the text.

Many thanks are also due to APA of Bologna for the material it supplied.

Photos: Piero Baguzzi

Graphics and paging: Amelia Verga and Paola Masera

© *Jocelyn Kerr Holding for the stencil drawings.*